AF605378

THE PHILOSOPHY OF HOUSEPLANTS

THE PHILOSOPHY OF
HOUSEPLANTS

SARAH GERRARD-JONES

First published 2025 by
The British Library
96 Euston Road
London NW1 2DB

ISBN 978 0 7123 5513 1
eISBN 978 0 7123 6844 5
Cataloguing in Publication Data
A catalogue record for this book is available from the British Library

Designed and typeset by Sandra Friesen
Printed in Malta by Gutenberg Press

For product safety information, please visit shop.bl.uk/pages/british-library-publishing, or the Publishing pages on bl.uk.

CONTENTS

INTRODUCTION

As I sit at my desk writing this book, glancing towards the window, I can see an old Christmas cactus that I bought after seeing it advertised on a well-known online auction site. Collecting it was an unexpectedly sombre experience – the house where it lived was being emptied, its owner having recently passed away. Walking into the now bare living room, I was struck by the visual silence of the empty space; and there, sitting alone in an old jardiniere, was the plant. I'm not ashamed to admit that the sight of it, forlorn and forgotten, made my eyes prick with tears. Its withered cladodes and drooping stems seemed to embody grief itself. I couldn't help but feel a profound sadness emanating from its very cells, as if it had absorbed the loss of its caretaker. It looked so vulnerable, and I quickly scooped it up, vowing to nurse it back to health. The thought of this old plant – likely more than 30 years old – dying after all the time and love poured into it was unbearable. For the owner, whoever they were, I would keep their memory alive by caring for this plant, nurturing it as they had.

Two years later, I'm relieved to see it looking better. Vibrant-green, plump cladodes now reach upwards towards the sunlight rather than drooping downwards towards the floor. The woody stems, once weak, are now rising with a new strength. Where once death seemed possible, life is returning. Yet, every time I look at it, I can't help but feel a little emotional and reflect on the deeper connection we share with plants. Why do we feel such a desire to bring them into our homes, to nurture them as we would a pet, marvelling at the milestones of a new leaf or flower, rather than simply viewing them as a source of food or oxygen upon which we are dependent for survival? To me this Christmas cactus has become more than just a plant – it's a living reminder of the bonds we form, the legacies we carry, and the quiet, enduring life that continues long after we're gone.

A POTTED HISTORY OF HOUSEPLANTS

HUMANITY'S CONNECTION with plants dates back to the dawn of civilisation, but the age of exploration, especially following Christopher Columbus's expedition, was the most revolutionary in the history of outdoor and indoor gardening. Landscapes and homes were irrevocably changed by the extensive plant migration between the Old World (Afro-Eurasia) and the New World (the Americas), which began in the late 1400s and continued in subsequent centuries. The movement of exotic plants across seas greatly benefited our scientific understanding of plant life and sparked a new curiosity and a sense of awe about the natural world. However, this era also highlights the complexities of humanity's relationship with plants and the profound damage colonial botany caused ecologically, economically and culturally – damage that continues to reverberate today. Many of these pursuits, led by 'plant hunters' celebrated for their bravery and botanical discoveries, exploited Indigenous people for commercial gain, stealing plants and ancient knowledge without recognition or compensation in a form of 'biopiracy' that created economic dependency while dismantling local industries. Botanists scoured lands for specimens to fill European gardens and museums, draining colonies of their botanical wealth while Europe gained scientific prestige. This exchange extended beyond outdoor landscapes, eventually influencing domestic spaces as these exotic plants from distant lands became symbols of wealth and status, with little thought given to the ethicality of these botanical quests. While the impacts of colonial botany, including biodiversity loss and the spread of invasive species, are challenges that we continue to address, this period also opened up a world of possibilities in terms of what could be grown both in gardens and our homes.

One of the earliest documented ideas for bringing plants indoors came from British inventor Sir Hugh Platt in his 1608 book *Floraes Paradise*: 'I consider it a most delicate and pleasing thing to have a beautiful gallery, great chamber, or other room that opens fully to the east or west, adorned inside with sweet herbs and flowers.' However, it wasn't until the eighteenth and nineteenth centuries, with great improvements in heating systems and a lucky accident in 1829 by Dr Nathaniel Bagshaw Ward, that growing tender tropical plants indoors would become not only possible but an essential addition to the interiors of Victorian homes. Ward, a trained physician with a deep passion for natural sciences, was also an avid gardener. Frustratingly, his

THE FERN-GATHERERS (IN AUSTRALIA).

attempts to grow ferns in London were repeatedly thwarted by the city's heavily polluted air. In his book *On the Growth of Plants in Closely Glazed Cases*, Ward vividly describes the conditions under which he struggled to cultivate his plants: 'The volumes of smoke issuing from surrounding manufactories, my plants soon began to decline, and ultimately perished, all my endeavours to keep them alive proving fruitless.' When he had all but given up hope of being able to grow ferns, he turned his attention to a sealed glass container in which he had placed a chrysalis of a moth together with some moist leaf mould. He observed that 'the moisture which, during the heat of the day arose from the mould, condensed on the surface of the glass, and returned from whence it came; thus keeping the earth in the same degree of humidity'. Then he noticed a tiny fern and grass growing on the leaf mould…

This seemingly simple yet groundbreaking observation revolutionised the transportation and cultivation of plants worldwide. Tender species that had previously died during long journeys across oceans were secured inside glass vessels, named Wardian cases, that helped to provide them with a stable microclimate. This innovation, which was little more than a miniature greenhouse, protected them from perishing and made it possible to ship them to botanical gardens and nurseries around the world, transforming the future of horticulture. Historian Keith Thomas notes in *Man and the Natural World: Changing*

Attitudes in England 1500–1800 (1983) that by 1839 nearly 18,000 imported plant varieties were thriving in England. With improvements in cast iron and glass construction, glasshouses were no longer exclusive to botanical gardens and professional nurseries; wealthy Victorian estate owners could now build their own, allowing exotic plants from tropical climates to flourish in their homes. However, such luxuries were out of reach for the average middle-class household, leading to the rise of indoor gardening, as people adapted by cultivating plants in their drawing rooms, lobbies and bathrooms. As houseplants grew in

popularity, Victorian homes turned into tropical gardens, with ferns, palms, begonias, aspidistras and orchids among the most prized specimens.

Due to a combination of Dr Ward's innovations and falling heating and glasshouse prices, gardening indoors became largely accessible to every level of the socioeconomic strata. This change ignited a new cultural obsession with indoor greenery. For the Victorians, ferns became the quintessential houseplant, sparking a phenomenon known as Pteridomania, or fern fever. This craze saw ferns adorn everything from homes to public spaces and even the fern-inspired design on custard cream biscuits, reflecting the growing obsession with indoor plants. A carefully curated indoor garden signified wealth, taste and refinement, but the practice, particularly for women, often went way beyond a hobby or mere decoration: it symbolised a deeper form of care and became a means of expressing nurturing instincts.

'Plant parenthood', a term popularised during the pandemic houseplant boom of the early 2020s, can trace its roots back to the Victorian era, when women often called themselves 'plant mothers', cultivating their plants with almost the same care and attention they gave their children. As Annie C. Brown, a contributor to *Ladies' Home Journal*, put it: 'I am a middle-aged woman with only one child, a daughter, who is grown up, so all my spare time is given to my flowers. They are to me as children.' This sentiment was widespread, with plants seen as extensions of the family.

Following the botanical fervour of the late nineteenth century, when Victorian interiors teemed with greenery symbolic of wealth and taste, houseplants began to fall out of fashion. The minimalist lines and streamlined aesthetics of 1920s Art Deco rejected the clutter of ornamental plants that had once dominated indoor spaces. This shift pushed many popular plants, including the once-ubiquitous

aspidistra, out of fashion. In George Orwell's 1936 novel *Keep the Aspidistra Flying*, the plant emerges as a potent symbol of middle-class conformity and the hollow pursuit of materialistic respectability. The decline of the aspidistra – and other houseplants of the time – mirrors not just a change in interior design but a broader rejection of the era's stuffy Victorian ideals, distancing itself in some respects from the associations with wealth and social status that these plants once embodied.

The decline in the popularity of houseplants was brief, and by the mid to late 1940s, indoor plants were poised for a resurgence. In the United States, low-interest mortgages offered to returning soldiers after the Second World War spurred a wave of suburban migration, and many families left cities for newly developed neighbourhoods. Suburban homes were larger than in cities, with more rooms and big windows, creating endless possibilities for incorporating plants indoors. Meanwhile, across the pond, British designers Charles and Ray Eames' iconic Case Study House No. 8 (1949), with prominently placed plants – including a striking giant monstera – and the design bible *The Architectural Review* featuring houseplants on the cover of its May 1952 edition, marked the official return of indoor plants as essential elements for the modern interior. And while the simple, sleek lines of mid-century modernism continued to make their mark across architecture and design, a more fun and frivolous fascination with Tiki culture also swept through the United States. Inspired by soldiers' tales of the South Pacific, many North Americans embraced the idea of creating tropical-inspired escapes at home. Tiki bars bedecked with tropical paraphernalia sprang up in homes, restaurants and lounges. Indoor paradises were brought to life with palms, philodendrons, bromeliads and strelitzias (bird of paradise), providing a welcome antidote for those working in towering steel skyscrapers.

As the mid-century progressed into the 1960s and 70s, attitudes towards plants and indoor spaces shifted, giving way to a more relaxed, organic, natural vibe influenced by rising counterculture and environmental movements. The 'back-to-nature' ethos of the era was in full swing, with houseplants becoming symbols of personal expression and environmental awareness and, for many, a means of creating a sanctuary amid the turbulence of social change. It was arguably the seventies which saw the emergence of the quintessential indoor jungle, a trend that brought macramé hanging planters, bottle gardens, *Monstera deliciosa* (Swiss cheese plants), Boston ferns, aloes, dracaenas and spider plants in abundance, capturing the era's laid-back spirit and at-oneness with nature. The 1970s marked a turning point in the history of houseplants, and they have since become a staple of interior design.

If the 1970s was the decade of superabundance, the 1980s interiors were defined by a go-big-or-go-home approach.

I remember fondly an enormous ceiling-scraping Swiss cheese plant my mum and dad had in their living room, whose aerial roots had burrowed their way underneath the carpet and along the entire length of the room. The decade of decadence drew inspiration from the grandeur of Victorian Kentia palm-filled parlours, mixed with the sleek, paired-back design of the Art Deco period. Monstrous

monsteras, bamboos, banana plants and huge *Ficus* took root in hallways. At the same time, a trend for cacti and succulents, which had begun in the early seventies, continued to develop on windowsills and in conservatories. Bold statement plants interspersed with chintzy fuchsia, jasmine, hyacinths, narcissus and geraniums signified a new trend for the heady scent and style of flowering plants. The eighties can't be defined by a single trend; it was a glorious, if often ridiculous, mash-up of styles, patterns, textures and colours, creating a visual riot of lush greenery and flamboyant blooms. Eighties interiors were unapologetically loud, a clash of cultures and a celebration of excess, with cascading English ivy spilling from twee wicker baskets, and tropical neon bromeliads perched on tiled bath surrounds like exotic trophies. Inspired by an affluence and bold materialism not seen in previous eras, there was nothing quiet or refined about this decade, but there was much to love about the creativity of indoor planting. *The Essential Guide to Perfect Houseplants*, written in 1984 by George Seddon, Andrew Bicknell and Elizabeth Dickson, illustrates the myriad styles of pots and planters used to display houseplants, ranging from Victorian-inspired Wardian cases and white jardinieres to Art Nouveau vases and antique bedpans. Tasteful, maybe not so much, but the 1980s were anything but dull.

The 1990s heralded the dawn of a new era of global connectivity with the introduction of the World Wide Web,

HOUSEPLANTS IN ANCIENT TIMES

Artefacts from as early as 4000 BCE depict the importance of plants and gardens in Persian culture, which drew inspiration from the four seasons and four elements – water, air, fire and earth – and provided an enclosed sanctuary for relaxation and contemplation. The simple yet symbolic cross design, which divided a garden into four areas, inspired the gardens of the Taj Mahal.

Pictorial depictions on frescos and archaeological discoveries reveal that the ancient Egyptians began incorporating plants into inner courtyards for decoration and display as early as 2000 BCE, also adorning temples and tombs with plants. Similarly, ancient Indian civilisations used potted plants in courtyards to enhance their living spaces.

The Hanging Gardens of Babylon (if they existed) were thought to be created by King Nebuchadnezzar II (reign *c.*605–*c.*561 BCE) for his wife, Amytis, and could be seen as an early example of biophilic design, incorporating planting onto balconies and the roof of a structure to help connect the occupants to the natural world. It is said that Amytis missed the mountains and greenery of her homeland, which is why the king created the gardens for her.

The Romans were adept at integrating nature within the confines of city life. City authorities housed residents in a type of multi-storey building called an insula, which often had a courtyard garden, or even a garden created inside a room. These gardens served as a refuge for the mind, body and soul, a place for exercise and religious rituals, or for pondering philosophy and literature. Depictions suggest that plants were also grown in clay vessels on the balconies and rooftops of the insulae, further adding weight to the premise that bringing the outdoors in was an essential and integral part of the lives of the Romans.

connecting us to a global community and revolutionising the way we communicated and accessed information and inspiration from around the world. This new period of globalisation saw an appreciation for Asian plants such as *Aglaonema* (commonly known as Chinese evergreens) and sparked a new-found obsession for orchids. These delicate and somewhat costly plants, once considered the domain of specialist growers, began to gain mainstream popularity. In his updated 1998 edition of *The New House Plant Expert*, the prolific author and gardening authority Dr D. G. Hessayon noted this shift: 'Orchids were regarded as specimens for the specialist grower in 1980 – now you can buy the easier varieties in garden centres everywhere.' Hessayon's guide not only catalogued the popular plants of the time but also offered valuable insight into the changing demographic of houseplant enthusiasts. 'For the first time,' he observed, 'we are buying more flowering plants than foliage ones, and the purchaser is more likely to be 20–30 years old than 45–55.' This shift in demographic marked the rise of a younger generation embracing houseplants as a lifestyle statement.

Interior-design trends of the noughties, particularly the rustic Tuscan style, perfectly complemented the use of ferns, palms, *Ficus* and even topiary in terracotta and faux-aged pots for an earthy aesthetic. At the opposite end of the scale, sleek, futuristic, artificial-looking environments left little room for nature. The 2010s ushered in the internet-driven trend of 'cottagecore', ironically emerging as a rejection of the trappings of modern living. This aesthetic celebrated a return to simpler times, drawing inspiration from traditional activities such as knitting, baking and gardening and romanticising a slower, more intentional way of life. The style embraced cosy comfort inspired by nature

and featured dried flowers, whimsical maidenhair and asparagus ferns, trailing ivy, and floral plants such as African violets. Simultaneously, the 2010s confirmed the arrival of the fiddle-leaf fig as *the* plant of a generation. No self-respecting millennial home was without a statement *Ficus lyrata*. Not the easiest plant to care for, and yet, despite this, it somehow became one of the most popular plants of the decade – a trend that has endured until the present day. Its popularity is perhaps best evidenced by the proliferation of plastic replicas, a poignant indicator of its enduring status.

More recently, the 2020s will undoubtedly be remembered for the pandemic and the consequential houseplant explosion which catapulted indoor plants into the stratosphere of interior design. The indoor jungles of the 1970s look deforested compared to the interior rainforests of 2020, when the maximalist approach to plants made a Gustav Klimt painting look positively understated.

As with most trends, historical, social and economic forces were at play. The pandemic disrupted life as we knew it, and in times of stress and fear, humanity instinctively turns to nature for solace. For many, that meant inviting a veritable jungle into their homes. Driven by social media, prolonged periods of isolation, and a desire for comfort and connection, the houseplant craze snowballed at an extraordinary pace, firmly establishing this era as one of the most important in the history of indoor gardening.

LEAF LORE

Before becoming fixtures on our windowsills and coffee tables, many plants we share our homes with held important roles in ancient remedies, superstitions and cultural rituals. Over time, they've featured in stories about healing, protection and prosperity passed down through generations and across continents. While houseplants are often seen as little more than decor, *Crassula ovata*, for example, holds a far deeper spiritual meaning in Chinese culture. Native to the xeric soils of South Africa, *Crassula ovata* was introduced to China in the eighteenth century, where it became known as the jade plant due to the colour and shape of its thick, glossy green leaves. As a precious stone, jade has long been an important symbol in Chinese tradition and ancient burial ceremonies, believed to help bridge the earthly and spiritual realms, ensuring a safe and peaceful passage to the afterlife. Over the centuries, jade has evolved to symbolise good fortune, health, wealth and prosperity.

You might spot a jade plant by the doorway when you visit a Chinese restaurant or takeaway. According to the principles of feng shui, a practice that governs spatial arrangements to enhance energy flow (*chi*), placing a jade plant in the foyer is believed to attract prosperity and financial success, welcoming wealth and good fortune into the space. The careful positioning of a plant beside the entrance is lucky for the business owner and the plant – many restaurants and takeaways have large windows to the front, which helps provide the plants with the light intensity they require to photosynthesise, and, as a result, they can be very long-lived. My local Chinese takeaway has a jade plant believed to be 75 years old, which puts on the most remarkable display of flowers each January.

Just as the jade plant embodies prosperity in Chinese tradition, *Dracaena trifasciata* – prized for its tall, sculptural leaves and ability to thrive in lower light – carries its own cultural significance in Afro-Brazilian religious communities. The symbolic importance bestowed upon the snake plant is rooted in the beliefs of the Yoruba people and the spiritual practices of Umbanda and Candomblé – traditions that emerged from the fusion of ancestral beliefs brought to Brazil by enslaved Africans with elements of Catholicism and Indigenous philosophies. In Brazilian folklore, the snake plant, also known as 'Sword of St George' or 'Sword of Ogum', is thought to ward off evil spirits. Ògún (or Ogum), the Yoruba god of iron, war

and hunting, is revered for his fierce, protective energy, offering guidance and strength in times of trouble. Orishas like Ògún are central to Afro-Brazilian spirituality; they are considered powerful, sentient forces that act as intermediaries between humans and the spirit world, imparting wisdom and healing and offering protection to practitioners. The snake plant's tall, sharp leaves represent a sword, making it a fitting symbol for Ògún and Saint George, who are seen as warriors and protectors. As such, *Dracaena trifasciata* is sometimes placed at entrances of homes to guard against negative energies, symbolically 'cutting through' or warding off harmful forces.

The power of the snake plant is not only harnessed for religious and spiritual purposes; the leaves are constructed from cellulose and lignin, which, once removed and dried, make a strong fibre for baskets, rope, clothing, fishing lines and bowstrings, thus earning it the other common name of 'viper's bowstring hemp'. Additionally, the juice or decoction from its leaves has been consumed for centuries to treat ailments such as gonorrhoea, earaches, toothaches, respiratory inflammation, flu, diarrhoea, coughs, haemorrhoids and influenza. Externally, it's applied to soothe bruises, sprains, wounds, abscesses, scabs, itchiness and ear infections and is valued as a natural antibiotic, hair tonic and pain reliever.

When it comes to houseplants with a history of curing ailments, though, few can beat *Aloe vera*. Records are found as far back as 1550 BCE in the *Ebers Papyrus*, an Egyptian medical papyrus of herbal knowledge, one of the oldest known medical works. The scroll contains 700 magical formulas and folk remedies to cure afflictions ranging from crocodile bites to toenail pain, and to rid the house of pests such as flies, rats and scorpions. It also sets out multiple aloe-containing preparations for treating external and internal ailments, including worms, headaches, chest pains, burns, ulcers, skin disease and allergies. From the Greek physician Dioscorides (born *c.*40 CE), who documented the medicinal properties of aloe in his work *De Materia Medica*, to Ancient Egypt, where it was revered as 'the

HOUSEPLANT MYTH-BUSTING

Whether you believe in myths and legends or not, some practical houseplant-care myths are best left forgotten and erased from history.

Ice cubes to water orchids

The best way to care for any plant is to try as best you can to mimic their natural growing conditions. Phalaenopsis orchids, native to tropical and subtropical forests in countries such as Indonesia, the Philippines, New Guinea and Australia, never experience freezing temperatures, so why would it be advisable to provide them with ice cubes? If you care about the longevity of your plants, don't shock them with freezing cold water. Instead, soak the orchid pot in water for 10 minutes, then let it drain.

Misting

The internet is full of suggestions about how often you should mist your plants, but have you ever stopped to consider why? To increase humidity? To make them think they are still in the rainforest? If you like doing it, by all means carry on, but the impact on humidity using a spray bottle is negligible, as are any other positive effects on your plant – other than perhaps helping to get rid of some of the dust that accumulates on the leaves.

Tap water is bad for houseplants

While rainwater is by far the best for houseplants, tap water, despite containing chlorine, is usually fine for most plants. This is because chlorine is one of the micronutrients required for metabolic function. Although tap water is considered safe to use on most plants, there are some exceptions, such as carnivorous plants, which are sensitive to the high levels of dissolved minerals in hard tap water.

Potting a small plant into a large pot will give it more room to grow

As tempting as it is, once your plant has grown out of a small pot to put it into the biggest one you can find, this isn't a good idea and can actually cause its demise. A small plant in a large pot will take longer to absorb water from the soil than a large plant in a small pot, and this increases the risk of the soil staying wet for a prolonged period of time, which can lead to root rot.

plant of immortality' and given as offerings at funerals or used in embalming rituals, *Aloe vera* has both physical and spiritual healing properties that have been used for centuries. Just as its leaves were used to heal wounds, aloe fibres were woven into cloth bandages and incorporated into the mummification process, symbolising renewal and the passage from death to healing and eternal life. Queens Nefertiti and Cleopatra were said to have used aloe gel as part of their daily beauty routine, adding it to baths and applying it to their face to keep their skin soft and youthful. Could there be more fitting icons to champion the remarkable properties of *Aloe vera*? To this day it remains one of the most commercially cultivated plants, used in drinks, beauty products and medicines. For some Egyptians, an aloe plant hung over the door of a new house is still believed to provide a long, fruitful life for its occupants.

While *Aloe vera* was thought to help provide a safe passage from death into the afterlife, the spider plant has long been associated with birth in folklore, witchcraft and herbal medicines. In Polish folklore, if *Chlorophytum comosum* produced flowers, it would signify either a family wedding or a baby's birth. Meanwhile, author Sandra Kynes, in *The Witches' Encyclopedia of Magical Plants*, suggests hanging a spider plant in the bedroom or placing one beside the bed to aid fertility. Beyond its symbolic associations, *Chlorophytum comosum* has been used medicinally for

centuries by the Nguni people during and after pregnancy. An infusion of the roots, thought to help protect both mother and child, is drunk daily by expectant mothers.

Across cultures, the plants we share our homes with have been intertwined with humankind spiritually and medicinally, their folklore revealing the power of plants to heal and protect.

BIOPHILIA

I AM USED TO BEING surrounded by plants at home, so much so that when I visit someone else's house or an indoor space without plants, it feels a bit odd. But why does it feel different to walk into a room with plants than without? Although we are not conscious of it, according to physicist Richard Taylor our minds seek out specific types of fractal patterns commonly found in nature that help reduce our stress response. He writes, 'Through exposure to nature's fractal scenery, people's visual systems have adapted to efficiently process fractals with ease … This fluency puts us in a comfort zone, and so we enjoy looking at fractals.'

The mathematician Benoit B. Mandelbrot first coined the word 'fractal' in 1967, describing a complex geometric pattern that repeats itself at different scales, meaning the whole structure is similar to its smaller parts. This is best visualised by looking at a tree, the shape of which is repeated in a branch and, smaller still, the veins on a leaf, and so it continues. Mandelbrot discovered that simple mathematical rules could be applied to things that look

Day & Son, Lith. to the Queen

IN-DOOR PLANTS.

Published by Smith, Elder & Co. 65, Cornhill, London.

visually chaotic and developed a theory of 'self-similarity' in nature, where the whole (e.g. clouds, fern fronds, mountain ridges, rivers, ocean waves, etc.) have the same shape as one or more of the parts.

By experimenting with MRI scanning, Taylor proved that mid-range fractals (those found in the natural world) engage the parahippocampal gyrus, which is involved in regulating emotions. Interestingly, this part of the brain is also involved when we listen to music. 'Your visual system is in some way hardwired to understand fractals,' explains Taylor. 'The stress-reduction is triggered by a physiological resonance that occurs when the fractal structure of the eye matches that of the fractal image being viewed.' When faced with more complex scenes, such as a busy city street, our brains struggle to process everything we see, leading to subtle discomfort. By contrast, we feel most at ease when viewing the natural features we evolved alongside, suggesting that part of our comfort in nature stems from the ease of processing these familiar patterns. As we surround ourselves with straight-edged, manufactured environments, we lose access to the natural fractal patterns that reduce stress through visual fluency. Alan Watts, the British-born American philosopher and lecturer, questions why we make everything rectangular, with straight lines, angles and order, when nature, including ourselves, is 'wiggly'. It's the wiggly that is familiar to us, which is maybe why I feel a certain unease when I'm in a room without plants. My brain is searching for comfort in the wiggly.

HOW TO MAKE YOUR HOME MORE WIGGLY

Most of us live in traditional boxy houses and apartments which weren't built with biophilia in mind, but you can change that by using these simple tips:

- Group plants together in odd rather than even numbers to make the overall effect look more natural. Experiment with plants at varying heights to break up a flat wall by placing them on shelves and windowsills, hanging them from the ceiling, and using plant stands to raise them from the floor.
- Incorporate natural elements and textures into a room. Choose products made from natural materials such as cork, rattan, bamboo, organic linen and stone.
- Maximise natural light by fully opening blinds and tying back curtains to the edge of windows. Take down any obstructions in front of windows (apart from plants) and move your desk closer to a window or skylight so you have a view outside.

- If you don't have a nice view from your window, add some pictures of landscapes and nature-inspired art to your walls.
- Use a colour scheme inspired by nature – think of forests, rivers, seas, sandy beaches, clouds and stones.
- Soften angular lines with irregular-shaped wall hangings and curved furniture.

Boxy rooms and straight, flat white walls are the opposite of wiggly. This type of unnatural environment deprives our senses of the organic shapes we are hardwired to recognise and find comforting. Biophilic design draws on the understanding that we function better when surrounded by nature and uses the theory of fractals to disrupt otherwise straight, angular, man-made surfaces and structures. As Rita Trombin states in her study 'Working with Fractals':

> Humans evolved in complex and sensory rich natural environments, where all of natural structure are fractals on a hierarchy of scales, from the large to the microscopic.... As people increasingly find themselves surrounded by urban landscapes, they become disconnected from

> nature's fractals and its stress-reduction qualities. This nature deficit can lead to an unhealthy build-up of stress, placelessness and sick building syndrome.

The World Health Organization first used the term 'sick building syndrome' (SBS) in 1983, in a report on how buildings can impact health. It describes situations in which the occupants of a building experience health and comfort effects that appear to be linked to time spent in a building, but where no specific illness or cause can be identified. The opposite of SBS is a healthy building, which among other elements, such as using natural building materials in its construction, incorporates a design that promotes a connection to nature, which helps support its occupants' mental, emotional and physical wellness. This can be making access to outside green spaces easier, or using smart lighting systems that connect with our circadian rhythm, as well as incorporating plants indoors to create the much-needed fractals that make us feel more comfortable. Office workers surrounded by plants are proven to be more productive and have fewer sick days than those working in offices without them, but only if the plants are healthy.

As much as I fully support the idea behind having plants in offices, there needs to be good care to ensure they survive. Office plants are often woefully neglected and become pitiful looking, which can defeat the purpose of making us feel happier and actually make us feel depressed, according to a study by the Royal Horticultural Society (RHS) and the University of Reading. The study investigated the psychological responses of 520 participants to images of twelve houseplants. All the plants were green except for a sad-looking palm with brown leaves. After looking at all twelve photographs, the participants were asked to say which was their favourite and least favourite and to rate each plant on a scale of ugly to beautiful, boring to interesting, depressing to uplifting, and unhealthy to healthy. They were also asked how beneficial they thought each plant was for well-being and air quality. It is no surprise that the majority of participants rated the neglected palm the lowest and thought unhealthy plants were not only depressing but worse than having no plants at all. There is a lesson for employers here.

Interestingly, the study asked the participants to rate the plants for air quality, which stems from a study done in 1984 by NASA to test whether plants could improve air quality in sealed environments such as space stations. The scientists concluded that plants could indeed improve air quality by removing volatile organic compounds such as benzene, formaldehyde and methylene chloride in controlled conditions. The last two words of that sentence are very important. This study was conducted in airtight chambers, vastly different from the conditions of an office building or house. One of the biggest misconceptions is that buying a houseplant will improve the air quality of your home or office. Researchers have since concluded that for air purification in real-world spaces, you would need 10–1,000 plants per square metre of floor space. So although there is truth in the fact that they can remove toxins, in an average-sized house in the UK you would need approximately 680 houseplants to even begin to make any meaningful difference to the air quality. Instead, the natural ventilation of buildings does the bulk of the work in removing toxins through open windows, doors, cracks, or air-conditioning systems.

Despite the questionable impact houseplants alone have on indoor air quality, the RHS study revealed that when we like the look of a plant, we perceive it to have a positive impact on our well-being. In the words of Dr Tijana Blanusa, who co-supervised the project, 'This research shows the psychological value of a simple houseplant in a situation where we know that individual plants' physical impact on indoor air quality may be limited.' Reinforcing the idea that it's not just about what plants do for us physically, but how they make us feel.

There is a vast amount of work to be done to realign and reconnect ourselves with nature, starting in schools, where the presence of plants not only creates a more inviting and stimulating environment for learning but is proven to enhance concentration, reduce stress and encourage creativity, via a complex series of effects on various neurological pathways in the brain. Nurturing a plant in

HOME, HEALTH
AND HAPPINESS
E.R.CROSSE

the classroom also teaches responsibility and respect for living things, restoring the connection between children and nature. In his book *Last Child in the Woods: Saving Our Children from Nature-Deficit Disorder*, Richard Louv highlights an urgent problem with the disconnection between children and the natural world, driven by social and technological changes over the past three decades. He argues that this 'nature-deficit disorder' leads to profound consequences, including 'diminished use of the senses, attention difficulties, conditions of obesity, and higher rates of emotional and physical illnesses'. Louv also warns that this disconnect 'weakens ecological literacy and stewardship of the natural world' needed to care for our planet, further compounding the problem for future generations.

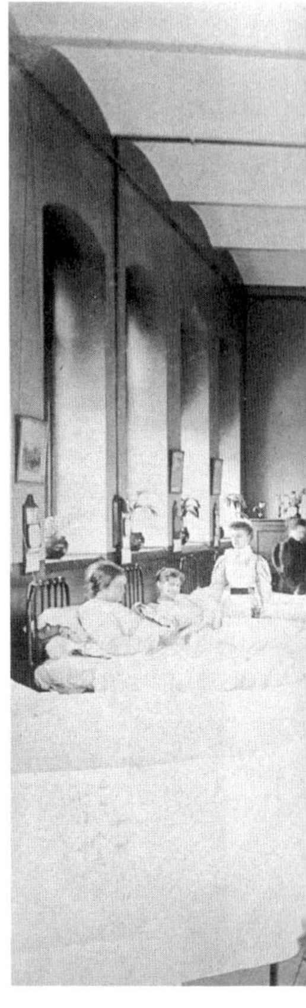

Addressing this disconnection is not only vital in schools but equally important in hospitals, where stress and anxiety run high. I have a very dear friend who was very fearful of her breast cancer treatment until she discovered that some chemotherapy drugs were derived from the yew tree. For her, being able to reframe the treatment as belonging to nature made it less frightening

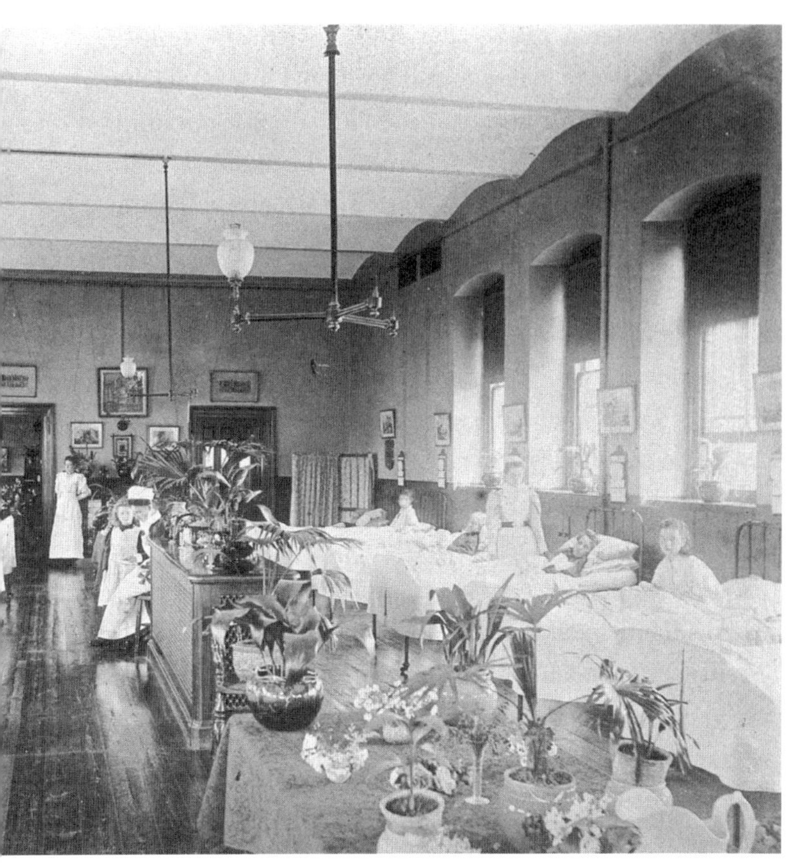

and connected her in a deeper way to the power of plants. I'd love to see yew trees planted outside oncology wards to help bring this connection to others experiencing a similar fear. As well as adding stress-reducing fractals to the sterile environment of wards and waiting rooms, having plants in hospitals can remind us that many of our medicines are derived from plants and highlight the symbiotic relationship between nature and healing. This connection can encourage hope and resilience in patients, reframing their experience of treatment as part of the natural world's ability to nurture and restore. Let's not forget the amazing staff working in hospitals and the benefits they could get from a tea break surrounded by plants rather than the bland, fractal-free, wiggle-less walls of the staff room.

In homes, classrooms, offices and hospitals the presence of plants can transform sterile, impersonal spaces into environments of growth, healing and connection. Investing in our well-being and taking meaningful steps towards rekindling our bond with nature needn't come at a great financial cost; in fact, it has been proven that incorporating plants into hospitals and offices actually saves money in the fewer sick days taken by employees. The question, then, is not whether we should invest in biophilic design but how we can afford not to.

OUTSIDE IN

Do you remember buying your first-ever houseplant? I wish I could say I do, but as it was well over thirty years ago, I don't know where or why I decided to buy it. Obviously, my ageing brain has chosen to discard this memory, or perhaps I don't remember because it wasn't a conscious decision to buy it. I know I must have been conscious when handing over money in exchange for the plant, but did I wake up that morning and purposefully head to a shop to buy a plant, or was it an impulse buy? Or an unconscious buy? At some point in our life, we've all impulsively purchased a jacket, top or pair of shoes, convinced it would make us look younger, cooler or more attractive, only to return the item a day later, realising we'd obviously temporarily taken leave of our senses. But what makes someone impulsively buy a plant? A plant won't change the way we look; it can, however, change the way we feel. Could buying a plant, therefore, be instinctive and evidence of something more profound in our psyche which instructs our feet to walk through the doors of a garden centre and march a plant to the checkout?

PLANT CATALOGUE 1901-02

NAIRN & SONS

CHRISTCHURCH N.Z.

Our brains are incredibly complex, containing roughly 86 billion neurons and an estimated quadrillion synapses (the minute spaces between neurons across which electric nerve impulses pass). It's no surprise that even after millions of years, we still don't have a comprehensive understanding of each individual neural pathway or the full extent to which our thoughts, emotions and instincts govern our actions and feelings. More than a century ago, Sigmund Freud added further complexities by popularising the theory of an unconscious mind – a second mind inside our own, if you like –that could be responsible for as much as 95% of brain activity, primarily unconscious and out of our control. Instinctual behaviours don't require conscious learning or thought; they are innate and lie within the unconscious mind. Perhaps, like newly hatched sea turtles heading towards the ocean, we instinctively head for the garden centre because our unconscious mind knows that surrounding ourselves with plants benefits our well-being … which could be a good excuse to use when your partner asks why you've brought yet another plant home.

The innate desire to surround ourselves with plants gave rise to the term 'biophilia', popularised in the 1980s by the biologist Edward O. Wilson, who suggested that humans have an inherent need to seek connections with nature. While I absolutely believe this to be true, the language around 'connecting with nature' inadvertently creates a false sense of division because we ourselves *are* nature.

So, the innate need for us to be connected with nature is to see ourselves as a part of nature rather than separate from it. This shift in mindset is supported by the profound effects even small exposures to the natural world can have on our well-being. As touched on in the previous chapter, many studies have been conducted about the outcome for patients in hospital settings exposed to plants, either in their rooms or with a view out of a window on to green spaces, versus those without. Each study revealed that patients able to see plants in their line of vision experienced stress reduction and had significantly shorter recoveries, less need for pain relief, lower levels of anxiety and fatigue, and more positive feelings about their hospital rooms, compared with patients without plants.

Our role within, and connection to, the wider natural world is not just psychological but physiological, woven into the fabric of our evolutionary origins. From the dawn of human history, our survival depended entirely on the resources nature provided. Plants were our food, medicine, tools and shelter, and this reliance nurtured a sense of safety, comfort and security. This connection, however, is under a great deal of stress and strain from the hectic lives we lead and our increasingly urbanised environments. While we are busy concerning ourselves with the trials and tribulations of life, our unconscious mind is also working hard to rebuild this connection. So next time you find yourself picking up a plant in a shop, perhaps don't question why; just know it's for your own good.

THE SCARLET
MEXICAN LILY
SEE PRECEDING PAGE FOR DESCRIPTION.

It's not only the loss of nature under layers of concrete that threatens to sever our connection with other living organisms but also our societal model, which works hard to redefine our role within the natural world, placing us above rather than among other planetary inhabitants. When we embrace our role within the intricate web of life, rather than separating ourselves from it, we rediscover a sense of belonging to a broader community, nurturing a more profound sense of purpose and self-awareness. In embracing our connection with nature, we can shift from exploitation to stewardship, helping to create a more sustainable and fulfilling way of living for ourselves and future generations.

Since the 1950s, doctors have prescribed antidepressants for symptoms of poor mental health. More recently, they have been writing 'green prescriptions', acknowledging that our increasing disconnect with nature has significantly contributed to the nearly doubling of global depression cases between 1990 and 2017. Rather than taking pills, a green prescription encourages individuals to spend time in nature to improve their physical and mental health. The idea is rooted in evidence that exposure to natural environments reduces stress, improves mood, boosts physical fitness and enhances overall well-being. Although nature-based interventions have only recently been adopted by medical institutions, the fundamental concept of green prescribing can be traced back to the Hippocratic era

PLANT ADAPTATIONS

Like plants, we adapt to our surroundings and respond to stressors that can affect our health. However, unlike sessile organisms, we are able to change our environment to better suit our needs and make ourselves happier. Houseplants, fixed in one place, cannot move but can respond to abiotic stress by adapting their morphology. The plants we label almost unkillable or easy to care for are simply those that are better able to adapt to the challenges of growing indoors than others. Plants in low light can create more chlorophyll to maximise their ability to capture sunlight. These plants will often look a darker green than those in brighter conditions. They can also bend their stems or reorientate their leaves towards a light source to harvest more light, in a process known as phototropism.

(*c.*460–*c.*370 BCE), when physicians suggested that the cause of most diseases was an imbalance of bodily fluids. The advice to regain balance was a change of habits and environment, which included, among other things, bathing in spa water and walking – not dissimilar to the advice recommended in today's green prescriptions.

Finding time in our busy lives to take a walk outdoors isn't always easy, and it's why bringing the outdoors in, as proven in the recovery of patients in hospitals when exposed to greenery, can offer similar benefits. From 2019 to 2021, sales of houseplants in the UK grew by over 50%. Can it be merely a coincidence that so many of us turned to plants for comfort during the pandemic? Or was this a clear example of our subconscious knowing what was needed to restore a sense of balance and connection during a period of great uncertainty?

Houseplants, even if we aren't aware of it, are more than decor; they reflect an extended sense of self, embodying our connection to nature and reinforcing our identity within the natural world. The simple act of caring for plants can be restorative, allowing the mind to focus on something other than the stresses of everyday life, and the importance of that cannot be understated.

Chronic stress has been proven to be one of the most common risk factors in 75–90% of diseases, including cardiovascular and metabolic diseases, neurodegenerative disorders and cancer. The vagus nerve, part of the parasympathetic nervous system, plays a vital role in helping the body to relax, shielding us from the myriad harmful effects that stress can cause. The nerve runs from the brain, branches through the neck into the chest, and ends in the abdomen. It is the longest cranial nerve in the body, part of the autonomic nervous system which

plays an important role in regulating mood and a whole host of unconscious tasks, including breathing, immune response, heart rate, blood pressure, digestion, taste, speech, and skin and muscle sensations. The polyvagal theory, introduced by Dr Stephen Porges in 1994, explains how the autonomic nervous system regulates responses to stress and safety through three key states: the ventral vagal (calm and connected), sympathetic (fight or flight), and dorsal vagal (shutdown or freeze). The theory suggests that when we perceive safety, our stress response decreases, allowing us to function more calmly and healthily. Conversely, when we sense danger our stress hormones are triggered, heightening vigilance, raising blood pressure and speeding up our heart rate. Our bodies sense many elements of modern life (primarily associated with artificial environments) as threats, such as loud noises, overcrowded trains, busy streets and congested roads, which sets off a stress reaction. These stressors in turn suppress the relaxing effects of the vagus nerve. On the other hand, natural environments help support the vagus nerve's calming and soothing properties, which dampen stress signals and contribute to a more positive feeling of physical and mental well-being.

Stress and mental illness brought on by our busy lives and a disconnect with the natural environment are recognised to be factors in the rise of chronic disease. Plants are a natural antidote for overstimulation and stress;

even just walking in a park, stepping into the garden or tending to plants on a balcony or windowsill can help counteract the impact of noise, screens and other stressors. With the average person spending 80–90% of their life indoors, the easiest way to experience the restorative power of nature is at home, where being surrounded by plants can evoke a subconscious sense of safety and well-being. Employers are also becoming more aware of the benefits plants can have on our health. Many are now turning to architects and designers who specialise in creating biophilic spaces to help employee well-being and productivity, transforming workplaces into healthier and more inspiring environments. It's clear there is an urgent need for us to realign ourselves with the natural world and explore ways of re-establishing our place within nature. If you've purchased your first houseplant – congratulations – your subconscious has already taken the first step in this significant journey. Now, it needs to be nurtured.

Cap. 60

Alsghelijcx zo vertrekent bo
caccius int zelue bouck van
den hondertich meulbiche
den. hoe dat bynnen der stede
van messine in ytalien eene
schoone maecht was. ghe
heeten lizabeth De welke huer drie broeders
die zy hadde ouermids haerer vrechheyt. ende
ghierichede : achter liden van huwene :
Ende alzo die drie ghebroeders eenen huer
facteur hadden van allen hueren zaken die
een zeere schoone ende behaghel jonghelync
was ghe heeten laurens Die huerlieden va
dere van jonx kinds beene up ghevoedt en
ghehouden hadde . zo ghebuerde dat hy ghe

PHILOSOPHY OF CARE

Human evolution is rooted in tribal communities where cooperation and mutual reliance are essential for survival, with each community member playing their part for the greater good of the tribe. Empathy and caregiving behaviours are deeply ingrained within the human psyche. Our children, born helpless and dependent, require years of care before they can survive on their own. Our instinct to nurture is fundamental to the survival of our species and helps explain our desire to care for living things, whether humans or the animals and plants with which we've evolved. Perhaps this instinct manifests as a gradual progression, starting with purchasing a plant, moving on to caring for a pet, and eventually embarking on raising a child. It's as though this progression serves as a practice ground to help build confidence and emotional readiness to take on the responsibility of nurturing a baby.

The act of caring is a win-win. Not only does it ensure the survival of our species, but when we undertake acts of compassion, we, in return, get a psychological reward in the form of a 'helper's high', likened to a mild hit of morphine, caused by a release of endorphins. I would argue that buying a potted plant is an act of compassion, for without someone to give it water, light and warmth, it will die. Much like a pet, a houseplant serves as a channel for our compassionate and nurturing instincts, offering the added reward of a dopamine hit when it unfurls a new leaf or produces flowers. Just like how giving a present is better than receiving one, the same feeling is evoked when our plant grows. We give them light, water and nutrients and in return they express happiness by growing. This reward for our time and care engages the same psychological pathways as acts of altruism, such as helping a friend or volunteering for a charity, albeit on a smaller, more personal scale. Looking after houseplants mirrors larger gestures of care while ironically, selfishly, providing us with the chemical release we crave. But caring for houseplants isn't just about the reward; they can offer us a sense of meaning and purpose.

In a study conducted in 2004 on the inclusion of indoor plants in a care home for people with dementia, 97% of the residents said they felt useful when nursing plants. This statistic is in accordance with a similar study by Erja Rappe and Aino-Maija Evers in 2001, which concluded that the act of growing plants may make older people feel needed. Scientific research has established that having a sense of purpose and feeling needed contributes to emotional well-being, particularly in later life. These studies also highlight how nurturing plants can restore a sense of responsibility in individuals who may feel disconnected or dependent. For dementia patients in particular, watering a plant can help with focus, contribute to a sense of identity and make people feel like their contribution is important. In this way, plants return tenfold the care they receive.

The ability of houseplants to offer emotional support isn't limited to the elderly. For many people, houseplants can provide companionship at home and extend to social communities where plant lovers gather in person or online to share tips, discuss problems and swap cuttings. The shared love of plants creates a network of care, in a similar way mycelium creates an interconnected web beneath the soil, linking trees and plants in a mutually supportive ecosystem. Without social connection, we become like a plant deprived of nutrients and begin to show symptoms of decline. Caring for plants cultivates a sense of belonging and shared purpose in an increasingly disconnected world, providing people with the mental nutrition they need to thrive.

Houseplants connect us both in the present and to the past. If cared for properly, plants can live for decades and, like a tortoise, even outlive their owner. An old plant stands as a testament to the years of love and attention invested in its care. When the owner passes away, the plant, if inherited by a friend or family member, becomes an embodiment of its previous caregiver, offering a sense of their presence and a reminder that, in some ways, they are still alive. Unlike a painting or jewellery, a plant serves as a living memorial. Each cell carries a connection to the past, and through its ongoing care, that connection remains unbroken. I know of someone who affectionately calls the Christmas cactus she inherited 'Granny', after her beloved grandmother who cared for the plant for over fifty years before passing away. The granddaughter now tends to this cherished plant as though she is caring for her grandmother herself.

While an heirloom plant is a deeply treasured memento for a grieving family, countless old plants have no one to be passed on to when their caregiver dies. I would urge anyone who loves plants to search second-hand websites for these old relics and consider giving them a home. After the years of care that I poured into saving the sad old Christmas cactus I rescued from a house clearance, it eventually bloomed, and it was one of the best 'helper's highs' I've had.

THE FUNDAMENTALS OF PLANT CARE

No one is born with green fingers or a black thumb. Those who seem to have a knack for caring for plants aren't magicians, just as those who struggle to keep them alive aren't serial murderers. The difference is simply down to an understanding of how plants function and a willingness to provide them with what they need in order for them to remain healthy. Most people would probably say I have green fingers, and yet I have killed lots of plants, but with each death, I've gained knowledge and an understanding of what not to do next time. If you repeatedly kill plants without learning from your mistakes, the cycle of buying and killing plants will continue. As this book is about the philosophy of houseplants, it's important to not only understand the hows but also the whys of plant care.

Light

Light is fundamental for plants; without it, they become unhealthy and eventually die. The priority for plants is the

RE-POTTING.

creation of food in the form of glucose, which they make through the chemical processes of photosynthesis. In the majority of plants, the role of absorbing light takes place in the leaves, which is why you might notice some houseplants orientating their leaves towards the window to maximise their exposure to light. Cacti (and other succulent plants without leaves) transfer the role of photosynthesis to their stems. Plants don't see light like we do; they sense it in photoreceptors. When pigments inside the plant are excited by light, it kickstarts photosynthesis, which leads to the creation of sugars essential for the plant to grow. If a plant is far from a window, it might not be able to sense the light; in turn, photosynthesis doesn't begin, and it will die a slow, hungry death. It might look nice in the corner of a room, but it won't look nice for long if it doesn't get the intensity of light needed to ignite the photosynthesis process. Signs that a plant isn't getting enough light include no new growth, small or yellowing leaves, spindly stems, and soil that stays damp long after watering. Essentially, a plant needs to be close to a window or underneath a grow light to create glucose.

Water

Plants don't drink water – it is pulled upwards through the plant in a process called transpiration, which is an unavoidable consequence of photosynthesis. Water is absorbed through the roots and then pulled up through the xylem (vascular tissue); it then escapes through tiny mouth-like openings called stomata, primarily located in the epidermis of leaves or stems. The pull of water from the soil is created by this evaporation, which leads to negative pressure (tension) in the xylem. Because transpiration is affected by many factors, such as light, humidity, air movement, temperature, substrate and stomata opening or

La terre.

closing, it is almost impossible to give blanket advice about when a plant needs watering. 'How often should I water my plant?' is a common question, but no one can provide a definitive answer, so it is best to ignore plant labels, apps and internet guidance suggesting a particular plant needs watering once a week. Strict rules can't be applied to watering, as many variables are at play; the type of plant, the size of pot and even the material the pot is made from (plastic retains moisture for longer than terracotta, which is porous) are factors in how often a plant might need watering. Where the plant is positioned also affects transpiration. A hanging plant will likely dry out faster than one placed on the floor due to warm air rising, causing moisture in the soil to evaporate quicker and transpiration to increase. Every plant in our home has a different watering requirement, so a one-size-fits-all approach isn't possible. The only person who can know when to water your plant is you. The best way to find out if and when to water is to push your finger into the soil and check for moisture, or weigh the pot in your hands. Picking up your plant and familiarising yourself with how heavy it feels after watering is an easy way to distinguish whether it needs water or not. If it feels very light, the soil is likely to be dry. If it feels heavy, there is still likely to be water in the soil and no need to add more. Familiarising yourself with how quickly the soil in a pot dries out is the best way to understand when to water.

Temperature

Many houseplants originate from tropical climates, making them well-suited to the average indoor temperature of 18–21°C. While some can tolerate a wider range of temperatures, they are less forgiving of rapid fluctuations, particularly cold draughts. Temperature plays a crucial role in photosynthesis; exposure to cold can slow a plant's ability to convert light into energy. Conversely, higher temperatures (if combined with bright light) can accelerate photosynthesis and the unavoidable loss of water through transpiration. This means that during summer, your plants may require more frequent watering compared to the slower growth conditions of winter. As the seasons change, it's essential to adjust how often you water. Always check if the soil needs water before pouring it in.

Substrate

The choice of potting medium for your plant is more important than it may seem. While plants require water and nutrients to thrive, they also need oxygen around their roots to function properly. This makes the texture and composition of the substrate an essential factor in determining the plant's overall health. Ultimately, what you choose to use should be informed by where the plant grows in the wild. Cacti and succulent plants tend to grow in xeric

WIRE POT FOR FERNS AND LYCOPODIUMS.

sandy, rocky soils, which aren't moisture-retentive, whereas carnivorous sundew plants grow in boggy ground. Most terrestrial tropical houseplants benefit from a substrate with larger and smaller particles (such as compost, perlite or bark), allowing airflow and good drainage. Mimicking the growing medium of the plant's natural habitat will go some way to helping it thrive in your care.

Fertiliser

Plants require macronutrients and micronutrients to grow. As the name implies, macronutrients are needed in higher volumes than micronutrients. Potassium, magnesium, nitrogen and phosphorus are among the most significant macronutrients for plants, while micronutrients consist of iron, zinc, manganese and copper (among others) and are used in much smaller amounts. Potassium, among other vital functions, helps regulate water movement and contributes to the plant's ability to fight disease; magnesium is crucial in the development of chlorophyll; nitrogen contributes to the structure of plant tissues; and phosphorus is primarily known for promoting root development, flowering and seed formation. Plants absorb nutrients from the substrate in which they grow; however, these vital nutrients and minerals are only available because microbes, bacteria and fungi help turn rocks and other matter into nutrients that plants can absorb. Microbes are microscopic but play an enormously important role for all living organisms, including us. Houseplant soils are usually sterilised to ensure there are no pathogens, but that in turn means there are no microbes for the plant to form a symbiotic relationship with. Consider using a soil inoculant containing beneficial bacteria and fungi to help the overall health of houseplants, and a fertiliser that helps feed not only the plant but the tiny underground helpers, too. As a guideline, fertilise plants when they are growing and not when they are resting (see Dormancy).

Dormancy

Seasonal changes, particularly winter (in the Northern Hemisphere), can have a profound effect on houseplants. In winter, when the Earth is tilted away from the Sun, we don't get as much light or heat, and the days are shorter. These signals can induce dormancy in some plants, which will conserve energy during this period rather than grow. If you notice a plant that has been putting out new growth during summer slowing down or stopping altogether, it is likely resting until more favourable conditions return. It's important to recognise this change and adjust your care accordingly. A dormant plant won't usually require as much water as it did when it was growing because photosynthesis has slowed. More houseplant deaths occur in winter than in summer, mostly due to too much water.

THE MYCELIUM NETWORK

When we think of mycelium, we most likely picture the fruiting bodies, which are the mushrooms visible above ground, and yet this is just a tiny part of one of the most extensive and incredible organisms on Earth. Beneath our feet is a vast network made from tiny threads of mycelium, which makes up a huge fungal web covering enormous distances. This remarkable network plays a vital role in keeping plants healthy, as fungal filaments intertwine with the roots of plants and trees, helping them absorb water and nutrients. The network also connects one plant to another, allowing nutrients to be transferred between them. In return for this service, the mycelium is offered a reward in the form of sugar and fats, a product of photosynthesis that the plant exchanges with the fungi. The largest network of mycelium was discovered in Malheur National Forest in Oregon, USA, covering 2,384 acres (about 3.5 square miles) and is thought to be somewhere between 2,400 and 8,650 years old. When I look at my houseplants imprisoned in their pots, I feel like I'm doing them a disservice. Thankfully, in recent years, the

benefits of mycorrhizal fungi have become part of the discussion about how we can improve our garden and indoor plant health, leading to the creation of inoculants which can add the fungi back in. I am an advocate of a holistic approach to plant care, believing that healthy soil leads to healthy roots and an overall better outcome. While the no-dig approach to vegetable growing, advocated by people such as Charles Dowding, is becoming increasingly popular, I would like the same thought to be given to our poor houseplants sat in sterile substrates, separated from their fungal friends that can improve their ability to resist pests and diseases, and increase water and nutrient absorption. Plants need the help of other organisms, in the same way humans need social interaction to thrive.

A plant that isn't growing also won't need fertilising as much (or at all) during this time. It is imperative to check the soil needs moisture before watering, as it can remain damper for longer during winter. Cacti and other succulent plants used to bright sunlight and warm temperatures are more susceptible to going dormant than other plants, and therefore particular care needs to be taken. I don't water my cacti at all from October to March/April, and I may only water other succulents once or twice during the winter. The combination of moisture around the roots and cold temperatures can be fatal for these plants.

MINIMALISM VS. MAXIMALISM

I HAVE OWNED A lot of houseplants over the years. At peak plant, I suspect I had somewhere between 300 and 400, believing that you could never have too many. I know now this is not true. Too many plants can have the opposite effect on well-being and, instead of being stress-relievers, become the source of stress. The need to water, feed and repot hundreds of plants while juggling work and family life can become overwhelming. Iris Apfel, the iconic fashion model, famously declared, 'More is more, and less is a bore', but when it comes to plants, there are practical considerations that can make the less-is-more philosophy appealing. I have to disagree that less is a bore. A single plant, in a beautiful pot commands attention, allowing for maximum appreciation of its form, colour and detail. It's also far easier to give one plant the care it needs than one hundred, often resulting in a healthier, more impressive specimen.

Minimalism gained popularity in the 1950s, originally used to describe art characterised by simplicity in shape, form and colour. This stripped-back aesthetic forced the

viewer to focus solely on what they saw in front of them, removing all other visual noise and disturbance, and the movement evolved over the decades to include fashion, design and lifestyle. While minimalism requires some restraint, it isn't about depriving yourself of things; it's about making intentional choices, ensuring each specimen brings joy aesthetically or emotionally. Every choice and decision should be meaningful; if I were to get rid of my entire collection and start again, I'd choose plants with unusual forms. I love cacti and succulents for their unique adaptations that have resulted in some of the most beautiful and strange-looking plants on the planet: *Cereus forbesii* cv. Spiralis with its extraordinary spiralling stem; *Lophocereus schottii* f. *monstrosus* (totem pole cactus) with bizarre geometric protrusions; or *Tephrocactus geometricus*, which looks like balls balanced on top of one another. It's these types of plants I'd place in my window in beautiful pots like works of art. The great thing about cacti and succulents is they don't need as much attention as tropical houseplants, meaning you can go on holiday and not worry about them being parched and wilted on your return.

A minimal-plant house can be far from empty and bare. It can become your very own art gallery where every plant and object is given the space to shine and be fully appreciated. By thoughtfully arranging your collection, you create a sense of balance and intention, allowing each piece to tell its own story. By sourcing special pots and stands

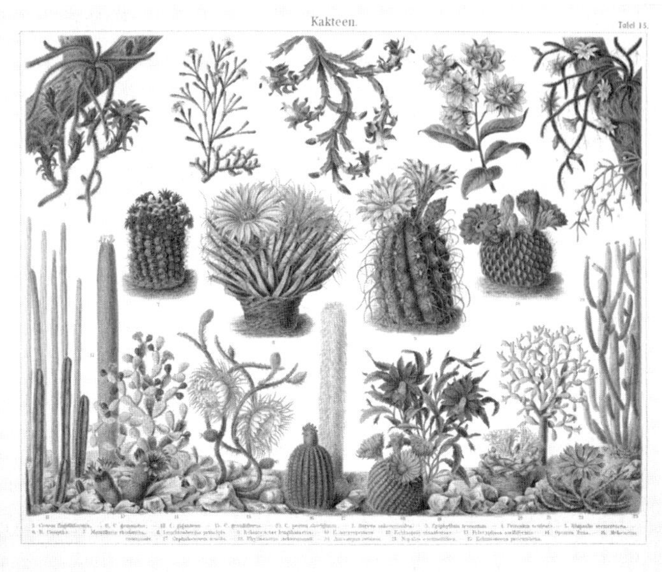

to complement each plant you can transform them into focal points, showcasing their beauty and individuality. Vintage websites, charity shops and reclamation yards sell unique accessories that can elevate a simple houseplant into an awe-inspiring design feature. To help keep plants looking their best, place them in a prime spot close to windows where they have access to the light intensity needed to thrive. A minimalist has no excuse for a neglected plant. Make sure they are dusted and pruned to help them photosynthesise and prevent them from becoming scraggly. Healthy, thriving plants are the ultimate testament to a minimalist approach.

In contrast, a maximalist embraces the philosophy of creative freedom and a more-is-more approach with unabandoned joy. The goal is not to curate but to create an immersive experience, akin to being in a jungle. Maximalism is a beautiful riot of chaotic harmony, where nothing is too considered or agonised over, and there is always room for just one more plant. A minimalist makes considered marks on a canvas, whereas, for the maximalist, their home is a canvas to be filled.

Creating an indoor jungle allows us to return to an environment that feels inherently familiar, a comforting cocoon that offers a sense of safety and protection. Beyond the undeniable benefits to our well-being, plants, like fashion, serve as a form of self-expression. They represent who we are and the story we want to tell. For maximalists such as the Victorians, rooms overflowing with plants symbolised wealth, status and sophistication. By the 1970s, however, the indoor jungle had become a statement of concern for the environment and a desire for oneness with the earth. Like painting, cultivating an indoor garden is a creative outlet, a canvas for passion, emotion and individuality. It's an unapologetic declaration that says, 'I don't intend to follow conventional rules', and a reflection of a vibrant personality that doesn't want to blend in.

My unintentional maximalist era wasn't so much about creating a jungle as it was a reaction to the waste and plight of plants thrown away for looking less than perfect. My

mission was to show others how easy it was to rescue them, but eventually I became engulfed and overwhelmed, and I began to adopt a more minimalist mindset. I looked at each plant individually, assessing its merits, and if it sparked joy, it stayed; if I felt nothing, it was gifted to someone else.

Paradoxically, minimalism can be maximalism; I maximised my free time by minimising my plant collection. Fewer plants meant fewer chores and more time to enjoy other things. Fewer plants also meant that for the first time, I could admire and appreciate each one. In an art gallery, paintings and sculptures aren't jumbled together; they are given space around them to breathe so the viewer can focus. Plants are comparable to works of art and, in giving them space, their beauty can be truly appreciated.

Maximalism is joyful and exuberant, without rules and restrictions, but can come with challenges. An indoor jungle can start to feel chaotic rather than calming. This is where you must be mindful of passion over practicality. Personally, I've found myself drawn towards a middle ground. I learned the value of restraint, not as a rejection of abundance (I still have hundreds of plants), but as a way to truly appreciate what I have. I will always love houseplants, but now I choose them more carefully, allowing myself the space to enjoy their benefits without getting bogged down with their care. The key lies in self-awareness: whether you're drawn to the peace and serenity of minimalism or the exuberance of maximalism, it's essential to choose an approach that works with your lifestyle. Plants are supposed to bring happiness and pleasure, not stress, so rehome those you don't want. If a plant no longer sparks joy in you, it will for someone else.

PRESENTATION

A PAIR OF SHOES CAN ELEVATE AN OUTFIT FROM understated to flamboyant, just as a hairstyle can be the fine line between fashionable and a fashion fail. Similarly, the way a plant is displayed can completely transform its impact within a room. While plants look great in terracotta, there are a myriad of ways they can be incorporated into interiors, with or without a pot. Their presentation can change how they are viewed, evoking emotion and enjoyment, and inspiring creativity in how we integrate nature into our homes and gardens.

The Chinese were trailblazers in the art of creatively displaying plants. *Penjing* (also known as *penzai*) is the art of shaping trees into miniature landscapes, depictions of which have been discovered in tombs from the Eastern Han Dynasty of 25–220 CE. The art of using earthenware vessels containing skilfully miniaturised trees is the precursor of Japanese bonsai, brought to Japan during the late Heian Period of 794–1185, and although it takes obvious inspiration from *penjing*, bonsai typically focuses on single or multiple

trees only. In contrast, *penjing* artists evoke feelings and emotions by often including elements such as rocks, water or figurines to create peaceful yet thought-provoking miniature landscapes which command contemplation. The Japanese also devised the art of *kokedama*, which involves encasing the roots of a plant within a ball of moss-wrapped soil, which negates the need for a pot. *Kokedama* can be displayed in a simple dish or suspended using wire to create floating orbs to dramatic effect.

Similar to the shallow dishes used in *penjing* and bonsai, bulb bowls were small, elegant vessels designed to hold heavily scented flower bulbs, which graced the interiors of affluent Chinese homes during the Yuan and Ming dynasties (1271–1644). By the eighteenth century, as the popularity of potted plants soared, these bowls evolved into a variety of stylish vase shapes. In the UK, however, Wedgwood put a whimsical twist on the traditional bulb bowl with the creation of the hedgehog pot. Crafted from black basalt, this hedgehog was planted with snowdrops or similar bulbs, allowing flowers to emerge through its pierced holes, creating both a striking and humorous display.

The Victorians, as we know, had a passion for opulence and extravagance, showcasing remarkable creativity in the way they displayed their indoor plants. Elaborate and intricately carved mahogany stands or jardinieres showcased their much-adored ferns, while tiered cast-iron plant stands and staging transformed their drawing rooms and conservatories into lush, theatrical jungles. These curated displays showcased their enthusiasm for indoor gardening, and elevated their plants, both figuratively and literally, into living works of art while also providing a conspicuous display of wealth and status to guests.

When I was a child, I used to create miniature worlds inside glass containers, filling them with plants, ladybirds, snails and other insects in much the same way as Dr Nathaniel Bagshaw Ward did in the early nineteenth century, when he accidentally created the first terrarium, or, as it was commonly known, the Wardian Case. As we saw earlier, in Chapter 1, aside from being a practical solution to transporting exotic plants across the seas, the cases were adopted by the Victorians to display ferns and orchids in their homes. Ornamental and more elaborate versions of the simple, sturdy cases used for shipping soon became a staple in stylish rooms across Europe and the United States.

After falling out of favour in the early part of the twentieth century, the terrarium made its comeback in the 1970s, reimagined with plants growing inside demijohns or carboys, typically used for fermenting beer. A further reincarnation of the terrarium appeared in the late 2010s in the guise of an IKEA cabinet that became popular on social media as a solution for larger humidity-loving plants too big to fit inside a terrarium.

In recent years, indoor water gardens featuring aquatic and semi-aquatic plants have gained popularity in the form of paludariums, a watery version of a terrarium. These displays create a veritable rainforest inside the home, providing the optimum growing conditions for terrestrial and aquatic plants. The calming combination of water and plants creates a soothing, anxiety-busting scene, making them a perfect antidote to life's stresses. Paludariums are often used to house small creatures and fish, adding to their sense of authenticity and charm.

COMMODITIES AND CONSUMERISM

According to a survey conducted in 2021, around 66% of American households own at least one houseplant, while in the UK in 2022, approximately 46% of Brits purchased a houseplant. It's fair to say that indoor plants have become a significant part of our lives and, as a result, their production has evolved into a highly specialised, intensive form of agriculture. These operations consume vast amounts of energy and water, spray harmful pesticides and often use peat-based soil, which devastates vital carbon-storing bogs, further exacerbating climate change. Similarly, the transportation of plants, often across continents, contributes to greenhouse gas emissions. However, with growing awareness, many producers are now shifting towards more eco-friendly practices, reusing or recycling pots and using greener energy and peat-free alternatives which are better for the environment.

Mass production undeniably has environmental consequences, but there's an additional layer of complexity in the houseplant trade: the impact on wild populations.

As rare, mature and exotic plants command a higher price tag, certain species face overharvesting in their native habitats, pushing some to the brink of extinction. Currently, three species of cycads, a plant that outlived the dinosaurs, are extinct in their natural habitat, partly because of our desire to have them in our homes and gardens. With many desirable plants, particularly those that are slow-growing as they can take decades to reach a decent size, it's a vicious cycle – the rarer they get in the wild, the more their value soars and the more they are ripped from the ground and sold. The Venus flytrap, native to the east coast of the United States, is vulnerable to extinction because of people taking them, as are many succulent plants such as *Dudleya farinosa* (bluff lettuce) and many species of *Conophytum*, 85% of which have been listed as either endangered or critically endangered by the International Union for Conservation of Nature (IUCN). However, there is hope. Global efforts are underway to combat plant poaching, a practice that not only endangers these species but also disrupts ecosystems vital to insects and animals. In 2020 Operation Atacama (named after the desert home to many endangered cacti) seized 1,000 of the world's rarest cacti, valued at over $1.2 million. This sting gained global media attention, highlighting the importance of conservation and the growing need to tackle plant poaching. Meanwhile, rangers in Saguaro National Park, Arizona, have been microchipping the iconic Saguaro cactus to deter poachers from stealing them. So far with positive results.

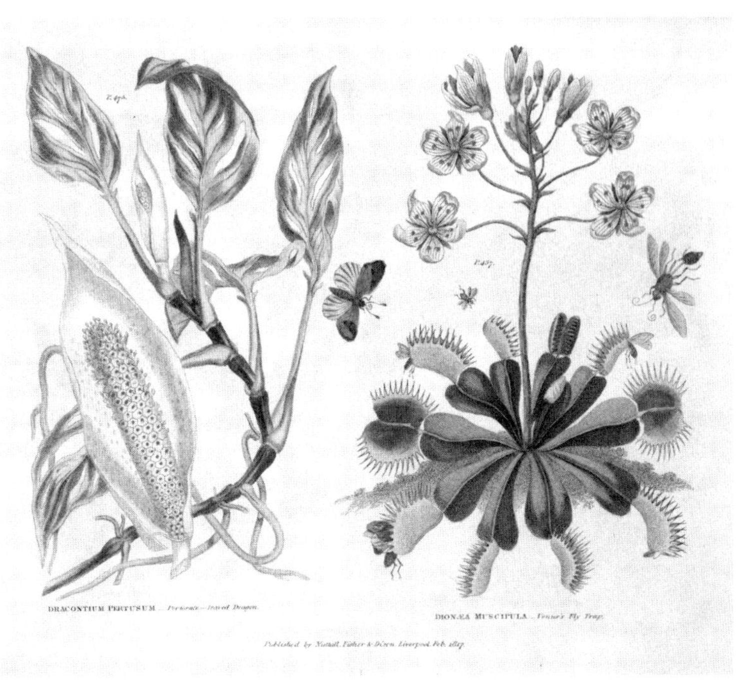

The popularity of houseplants reached unprecedented heights during the COVID-19 pandemic, when demand soared and an infatuation with rare plants pushed their prices up beyond what most could have imagined. In 2021, extraordinary sales captured global attention, such as a white variegated *Rhaphidophora tetrasperma* auctioned in New Zealand for nearly $20,000, and a variegated *Monstera adansonii* sold on eBay for $38,000. These astronomical prices reflect a growing fascination with rare plants but also highlight a shift where some plants are valued more for financial gain than their ecological role.

The trend for buying plants as status symbols or investment pieces raises questions about the balance between our love for plants and the sustainability of the hobby. What began in ancient times as a way to decorate our homes and bring nature indoors has spiralled into an industry that sadly sometimes prioritises profit over preservation.

The internet and social media have revolutionised plant collecting, making it easier to discover and acquire

plants from around the world. These platforms have helped to inform, inspire and connect a passionate community of plant enthusiasts across the globe. However, they have also unintentionally fuelled a market for rare and illegally sourced plants, adding to the challenges faced by conservationists and, in some cases, impacting vulnerable ecosystems.

But it would be wrong to solely blame plant lovers or social media for the rise in poaching. It's a highly complex issue involving economic, social and environmental factors such as unemployment and poverty, especially in rural communities where work is scarce and wages are poor. The issue is multifaceted and is as much about the human desire to own rare plants as it is about governments and capitalism. The demand for 'special' plants certainly incentivises poaching, especially when rare plants are seen as symbols of status or exclusivity. However, socioeconomic issues and the need for more regulation or enforcement in some regions allow the illegal plant trade to flourish, making it difficult to protect endangered species effectively. Economic hardship in these areas exacerbates the issue, as people may feel they have little option but to turn to plant poaching to feed their families. Systemic change, global cooperation and individual responsibility all play their part in ending the scourge of illegal poaching, but awareness of the issue is the first step in the battle to save what is left of our rapidly dwindling plant population. So before buying a plant, particularly online, there are some signs you should look out for so you can be sure that you aren't contributing to the problem.

Pay particular attention to photographs. Plants from nurseries don't usually have imperfections in the same way as plants in the wild do. Mass-produced plants are raised in ideal conditions, whereas those in nature have suffered all weathers, which will be evident in their appearance. Wild-collected plants often have irregular shapes and may have scars, and the roots could show signs of damage. The plants offered for sale may be photographed in their natural habitat or bare-rooted (without a pot). If you are concerned in any way about the appearance or have doubts about the plant's origins, ask the seller questions. If the answers don't convince you or if the seller avoids answering questions, trust your instinct and don't buy it. It would help if you also made the website or social media platform aware of your suspicions so they can remove access to sellers suspected of plant poaching. If purchasing a plant from overseas, it must come with a phytosanitary health certificate, and if the species is CITES-listed, CITES permissions must be obtained before shipping live plants abroad. A reputable seller will be upfront about the time and money required for this. Be aware of the location

FOR THE LOVE OF BOGS

Peat bogs, formed over thousands of years, are one of the rarest habitats on earth, covering just 3% of the world's land surface, but are one of the most significant in the fight against climate change. In a typical ecosystem, plants die and decompose, releasing carbon back into the atmosphere, but in a waterlogged bog, decomposition slows significantly and, over the years, layers of carbon-rich peat are formed. In the UK alone, bogs 'lock in' an estimated 3.2 billion tonnes of carbon. The sequestered carbon is released back into the atmosphere when we disturb the peat through excavation. Peat bogs need protection, not only for the plants, animals and insects that rely upon this unique habitat for survival, but also to preserve their role as a natural carbon sink, helping to fight the impact of climate change. Always choose peat-free potting compost and help keep peat where it belongs, in bogs not in pots.

of sellers and steer clear of anyone who claims quick international delivery without being transparent about the necessary permissions and procedures.

If you want to be more sustainable when it comes to cultivating your houseplant collection, there is no better (or more rewarding) way than propagating cuttings from your own plants or from friends and family. With the rise in the popularity of houseplants has come a wealth of innovative ideas for indulging our passion without harming the planet or our bank balances. Join online plant exchange groups or look out for in-person plant-swap events in your area. Search online second-hand sites for plants looking for new homes; you can find some amazing, characterful plants for a fraction of what they would cost new. But I certainly don't want to discourage buying from plant shops and garden centres – supporting local, responsible plant retailers is essential – perhaps just look for those with policies to reduce waste, avoid peat-grown plants and support local growers. Every small change helps.

PLANT RESCUE

In a world where everything must be flawless, from our faces to our curated lives on social media, imperfection has become something we are uncomfortable with, something to be ashamed of, to hide, avoid and discard. Almost everywhere we turn, we are bombarded with images of unrealistic ideals and values, fuelling a consumptive course through life and leaving a wake of destruction behind us. But what if we saw beauty in imperfection instead and, like the ancient Japanese philosophy of *wabi-sabi*, embraced the story behind the broken, wilted and scarred? Never have we generated, desired or possessed so much stuff – unlike previous make-do-and-mend generations, we live in a time of abundance, encouraged to throw away and buy more – but this can provide us with a unique opportunity to rethink how we value what we own. By caring for what we already have, we can help reduce waste and protect the planet from further damage.

Behind the glass windows of commercial greenhouses, garden centres, shops, warehouses, supermarkets and homes, plants with 'imperfections' are thrown away in their millions worldwide, along with the soil, pot and all the resources used in the process. As soon as orchid flowers begin to wither, the plants are often promptly binned, despite them still being very much alive. One of the most exciting things about gardening is watching flower buds appear and then bursting into bloom; therefore just after the orchid has finished flowering is, in fact, the perfect time to buy it! Nurturing an orchid, particularly one that would have been thrown away, and watching it flower again brings with it a sense of pride and joy, which can be addictive. Not only do I love the feeling of watching a plant recover or flower again, but it's also a practical way to learn about their care. A neglected or flowerless plant can be a great teacher, allowing us to take risks and experiment in a way we might not want to with a healthy plant.

In many cases, an ailing plant can grow to be healthy again by cutting it back or, in the case of an orchid, fed, watered and put on a windowsill until it has the energy to rebloom.

In his philosophical and playful manifesto *The Nation of Plants: A Radical Manifesto for Humans* (2022), Stefano Mancuso writes, 'We exist thanks to plants, and we will continue to be able to exist only in their company.' In our busy, technologically overcrowded lives, it is all too easy to forget that our entire survival is reliant upon plants. Every breath we take, all we eat, our medicines, skincare, clothes and even building materials depend on plants,

PHALÆNOPSIS VEITCHII

FLORAL MAGAZINE NEW SERIES

HOW TO GET AN ORCHID TO REBLOOM

I never buy orchids in full bloom. I only buy them when the flowers are withering, primarily to save them from being thrown away but also because they are often reduced in price. If the flower stem is green, I cut it beneath the lowest flower and above a node (small bump on the stem). By doing this, the plant can often regrow a secondary flower stem from the node and bloom again fairly swiftly. If the stem is brown, I cut it off at the base.

Keeping the sticks that hold the flower stem upright isn't necessary. They are used for transportation to ensure the flower stem doesn't break, to save space and to hold the flowers in an upright, unnatural way. Take them away and allow the flower stem to regrow in any way it wishes. Here are three simple tips to help encourage a Phalaenopsis orchid to rebloom:

- Position it on a windowsill where it receives direct sunlight for only a few hours a day;

don't place it next to a window that has direct sunlight all day long or it can burn the leaves.

- Don't water without checking the colour of the roots – these will tell you when they need to be watered. Green roots are hydrated and don't need water; silver-coloured roots need to be watered. To water, place the plastic pot into a decorative pot and fill the outer pot to the top. Leave to soak for 10 minutes before draining the water. Add fertiliser once every few weeks.
- A drop in temperature of 8–10°C at night can help encourage blooming.

but somewhere along the line, we have lost sight of their crucial role in our lives. This phenomenon, known as 'plant blindness', was coined by botanists J. H. Wandersee and E. E. Schussler in their 1999 article 'Preventing Plant Blindness', and can be simply defined as an inability to notice or appreciate the importance of plants in our environment. The casual discarding of plants at the first sign of imperfection – a brown or yellow leaf or a faded flower – reflects a side of our culture that is increasingly disconnected from nature, but it can be something as seemingly insignificant as saving a plant that offers us an opportunity to reconnect with the natural world. Nature didn't evolve to be perfect; plants function to the best of their abilities for survival, which, on a shop shelf or inside our homes, can be tough, given that the conditions are far removed from their natural habitats. Instead of tossing them away when they don't look perfect, nurturing them back to health or encouraging them to rebloom is a small yet significant way of acknowledging the vital role they play in our lives.

Plants understand the art and beauty of imperfection like no other. When you go for a walk, you will see leaves with rips, scars and holes, as well as twisted stems and broken branches. These are not defects; they have a story to tell of wind, sun, rain, frosts and predators. Such resilience should not be rewarded with disappointment or impatience but seen instead as a reminder of a plant's will to survive and an opportunity to delve deeper into understanding its needs. By caring for plants through their ups and downs, we can gain a deeper connection and respect for nature.

The pile-them-high-sell-them-low concept seen in supermarkets poses a difficult challenge for me. While on the one hand, I disagree with the selling of plants in places that don't care for them; on the other hand, I can't bear to see them dying from neglect, and so I feel compelled to save them, thus resulting in a sale for the supermarket. I wholeheartedly agree that plants should be accessible to all and that they should be affordable, but at what cost to the environment when so many millions are grown only to end up dying on the shelves and being thrown away along with their plastic pots, which will still be polluting the planet in 500 years' time? The issue extends beyond individual plants to the environmental toll of mass production, which generates immense waste, from plastic to the resources used in cultivation and transport. But the loss is not just environmental; it's a lost opportunity for connecting with the natural world and appreciating the slow, rewarding process of nurturing a plant.

How might our relationship with nature change if we saw each plant as a long-term commitment rather than a fleeting novelty? (Spray-painted cactus with googly eyes, anyone?) If cared for properly, houseplants can live for decades and even outlive us, becoming an heirloom for future generations. The world's oldest pot plant, an Eastern Cape giant cycad, resides at Kew Gardens, weighs over a ton, is approximately 4 metres tall and is an astonishing 245 years old. I was once asked to rehome a cactus estimated to be 120 to 150 years old after its owner sadly passed away. Handed down through the generations, this remarkable plant likely began growing during the reign of Queen Victoria and has endured through two world wars. Indoor plants that have lived for over a century are not

uncommon and are living proof of what patience, love and care can do, but not every plant is lucky to experience such devotion. So many are tossed away when they no longer look as good as they once did. Our throwaway culture is often fuelled by misinformation or an unwillingness to take the time required to nurture a plant back to health or help it bloom again. To rescue a plant is an act of empathy and a quiet protest against the disposability of modern life. It challenges us to look beyond the superficial, reject the hopeless pursuit of perfection, and invest time in nature and ourselves. In saving a plant, we also save a part of our humanity.

FURTHER READING AND SELECTED REFERENCES

Books

Richard Louv, *Last Child in the Woods: Saving Our Children from Nature-Deficit Disorder* (2005)

Stefano Mancuso, *The Nation of Plants: A Radical Manifesto for Humans* (2022)

Benoit B. Mandelbrot, *The Fractal Geometry of Nature* (2021)

Jared D. Margulies, *The Cactus Hunters: Desire and Extinction in the Illicit Succulent Trade* (2023)

Florence Williams, *The Nature Fix: Why Nature Makes Us Happier, Healthier, and More Creative* (2017)

Edward O. Wilson, *Biophilia* (1984)

Websites

Wildfowl and Wetlands Trust: wwt.org.uk/discover-wetlands/wetlands/peat-bogs

Journal of Biophilic Design: journalofbiophilicdesign.com

Studies and Articles

Bill B. Baumann, 'The Botanical Aspects of Ancient Egyptian Embalming and Burial', *Economic Botany* (1960), Volume 14, Issue 1, pp.84–104

Erja Rappe and Leena Lindén, 'Plants in Health Care Environments: Experiences of the Nursing Personnel in Homes for People with Dementia' (2004)

Rita Trombin, in collaboration with Terrapin Bright Green, 'Working with Fractals: A Resource for Practitioners of Biophilic Design' (2020)

R. P. Taylor, B. R. Newell, B. Spehar and C. W. G. Clifford, 'Fractals: A Resonance Between Art and Nature', *Mathematics and Culture II* (2005), pp.53–63

R. P. Taylor and J. C. Sprott, 'Biophilic Fractals and the Visual Journey of Organic Screen-savers', *Nonlinear Dynamics, Psychology, and Life Sciences* (2008), Volume 12, No.1, pp.117–129

LIST OF ILLUSTRATIONS

All images from the collections of the British Library unless otherwise stated.

p.19 A potted *Ficus lyrata*, or fiddle-leaf fig tree. (www.123RF.com)

p.22 Ornamental foliage: *Croton variegatum*, *Vriesta speciosa*, *Dracaena maculata*, *Dracaena terminalis*, *Pavetta borbonica*, *Haemadictyon venosum*, *Begonia splendida*, *Coccocypselum repens*. Plate from *The Illustrated Bouquet*, Edward George Henderson, London, 1857–1864.

p.24 House of a Chinese Official, from a collection of Chinese watercolours, *c.*1800–1805.

p.29 Aloe. Plants copied from nature in the Roman States, by Gerardo Cibo, *c.*1564–1584.

p.30 Spider plant in macramé plant pot holder. (www.123RF.com)

p.32 Frontispiece to *In-door Plants, and How to Grow Them, for the Drawing-room, Balcony, and Greenhouse*, by E. A. Maling, London, 1862.

pp.34–35 'The Causeway', James Parmelee House, 3100 Macomb Street, Washington D.C. Photo by Frances Benjamin Johnson, 1919. (Library of Congress, Washington, D.C.)

p.41 *Home, Health and Happiness*, by the Bile Bean Manufacturing Co., London, *c.*1900–1909. (Wellcome Collection)

pp.42–43 The Royal United Hospital, Bath. Photograph, *c.*1870. (Wellcome Collection)

p.46 Nairn & Sons Ltd., plant catalogue 1901–02. (Alexander Turnbell Library, National Library of New Zealand)

p.49 'The Scarlet Mexican Lily', seed catalogue of Dingee & Conard Co., 1897. (Smithsonian Libraries and Archives)

p.53 'The Balcony and Window Garden', from *The New Practical Window Gardener* by John R. Mollison, London, 1877.

Also available in this series